Thomas Townsley

TRISTAN CHORD

SurVision Books

First published in 2026 by
SurVision Books
Dublin, Ireland
Reggio di Calabria, Italy
www.survisionmagazine.com

ISBN: 978-1-912963-62-1

Acknowledgments

Grateful acknowledgment is made to the editors of the following, in which some of these poems, or versions of them, originally appeared:

Doubly Mad: "Death Rattles" (fragments)

Lotus Eater: "Fourteen Septets Suspended in a Tristan Chord"

Contents

Fourteen Septets Suspended in a Tristan Chord 5
Death Rattles 10
Searching for *Le Mot Au Jus* 33

Fourteen Septets Suspended in a Tristan Chord

1.

Stir up bits from the bottom; watch them float in tepid broth.
Always disambiguate the mountain laurel.
When observing how far your wake trails behind you,
try to feel at peace.
Remember that allegory has the potential for excess,
but do not spare the ampersand on that account!
Beware asphyxiation by mirror.

2.

What these rhizomes need is a piano repairman!
I looked her smack dab in the corolla.
"How about some radical mimesis?" I purred.
Tonight's moon is made of memory-foam.
The new restaurant caters to narcoleptics—
reservations recommended!
When thinking of silence, consider the page you write on.

3.

This creamy-white species has waxy, pale green or pinkish bracts.
As a narrative, it was fairly conventional.
The specific epithet *'fontinalis'* comes from the Latin for "of a spring or
fountain."
Some maintain that superior literary forms are organically unified.
One can see right away that the expressionist elements—
the lobotomizing mitre and talking cuttlefish—are beginning to find a
new space.
"The beginning of the poem is just whiteness," he insisted.

4.

Is that a new hurdy gurdy in the mezzanine?
Is William Dean Howells still considered a "major realist"?
Who sneezed on the tabula rasa?
Why do all these sou-chefs have furrowed brows?
How did the stranger with burnt fingertips dedicate his life to Eros?
Has anyone found the hidden levers?
Where does this cul de sac lead?

5.

Active voice is what you should use.
Our herd instinct was deactivated by the woman in the floppy hat.
Payment must be remitted before the whirlybird falls into desuetude.
The sinkhole was occupied by three bankers in powder blue suits.
"These sutures had to be made by somebody!" is what she shouted.
A monogrammed yoyo was presented to the birthday boy,
but a trapezoidal swath of radical mimesis was his true desire.

6.

It is easier to predict which tentacle a cuttlefish
will use to make the sign of the cross
than it is to define "radical mimesis."
I am insufficiently photo-optic—so the mirror tells me.
One of my former lovers is now the world's foremost collector of tiny
    clocks.
"It doesn't matter what you order," the waiter said.
"You'll be asleep by the time it gets here."

7.

"...the people who have been brought up on the ideal grasshopper, the heroic grasshopper, the impassioned grasshopper,
the self-devoted, adventureful, good old romantic cardboard grasshopper, must die out before the simple, honest, and natural grasshopper can have a fair field,"
William Dean Howells wrote in *Criticism and Fiction,*
using an extended metaphor and personification to advocate for realism.
The allegorical mind takes sides with the object.

8.

Gall of the Earth is to Mountain Laurel as William Dean Howells is to a cuttlefish.
Mirrors are not predisposed to narrative, but tiny clocks are.
Did I mention that the mitre's top is said to resemble a fish's mouth?
Our cul de sac was overrun with brook trout.
After dessert, we'll wake up to some maniacal wheel fiddle music!
The stranger with burnt fingertips travels the Jersey coast, setting carousels on fire.
Three bankers genuflect to a hand-held potato masher.

9.

Gelatinous tears were wept by the piano repairman.
An augmented fourth, augmented sixth, and augmented ninth above the root note are the intervals of which the Tristan chord is comprised.
Having his desire laminated was another gift the birthday boy received anonymously.

My leitmotiv was fumbled by the trombone section.
What remains permanent is the concept of “is.”
That lever was first pulled by a one-eyed panegyrist in 1974.

10.

Did you solve the tangram puzzle?
Is there any place darker than the inside of a mirror?
Is that man with burnt fingertips about to enter our cul de sac?
Why does the moon say “was” but never “is”?
Did the buck-toothed narrator leave these phenomenological shower curtains behind —or was it the reader, still glistening with allegory?
Who opened the window and let these ideal grasshoppers in?

11.

I hid this Gall of the Earth with its drooping bells behind the tabula rasa, intending to surprise you, but the spiteful mirrors gave us away.
“I much prefer mountain laurel,” you said. “It’s not so allegorical.”
Now the vinaigrette casts a veil of lethargy upon us.
In the background, too many clocks are ticking.
“Can one play a Tristan chord on the hurdy-gurdy?” the waiter asks, dispensing the mashed potatoes. .

12.

A whirly-bird piloted by three bankers drops potato mashers on the cul
de sac.
The brook trout’s markings—worm-like vermiculation and red dots with blue halos—read like ineffable symbols transcribed from a poem
dictated in a dream.

“Excuse me, waiter—and pardon me for asking—, but what happened to your fingertips?”
The ineffable is always embodied.
“Who reframed my corolla?” she squeaked, radiant in moonlight.
Ordinary language does not use itself to reflect on itself.

13.

The waiter set a plate of steaming calamari on the tabula rasa before him, but William Dean Howells did not stir from his slumber.
Instead, he dreamed that he knelt in a sinkhole beside three bankers in powder-blue suits who communicated using an insect-like language he could not understand—as if their voices were filtered through a Waring blender that alternated constantly between “Chop” and “Puree.”
“If I could acquire this language and translate it into works of fiction,
I would be the greatest writer of my generation,” he thought—
failing to notice the potato masher.

14.

Do not look the panegyrist directly in the eye.
Order your trout almondine “to go.”
Remember, the mountain laurel is toxic in all its forms, from leaf to
stem to branch.
Pay the piano repairman in cash.
Tell yourself “Radical mimesis made me what I am today.”
As you stare deeply and lovingly into the mirror,
stir up bits from the bottom; watch them float in tepid broth.

Death Rattles

1.
Just keep talking. They can't stay mad forever. Paste egg cartons to the walls for better acoustics. Stir soup desultorily. One of your better angels is wielding a hammer. How far does this extension cord reach? Some predators detect movement rather than the prey itself—dear Reader, take note. I'd be all right if it weren't for this singing rash, but then, most stories end badly, don't they, little Kite Tail? I'm cutting back on salt. I'm kicking my props to the curb: my stiletto gaze, my moon ladle, my chess manual on the Blackmar-Diemer Gambit, my verbal pontoons... Maybe Joseph Cornell can put them to use in one of his "clever arrangements." Last night, I dreamt of you, and it wasn't "surrealism," though to be fair, when I pronounce "surrealism," I hold the "m" for at least five seconds, waiting for the pink rats to pass. This extension cord is becoming problematic—I think it reaches further than we thought. May I still say "we"? Is that a claw or a ball peen hammer? What time does everyone around here go to bed?

2.

The weeks have eaten. The exhaust pipes committed suicide and disappeared, like spokesmen upon the veiled balconies of television. Hooves in the dew scattered brain stems, and I followed. Now I'm told to be alert for hidden lizards and overflowing quattrocentos. Caves and silences portend some sort of besmirching, and yet "Observest thou her Aristotelean hem line?" Vinyl sky. The bottom of a blue wind. A corybantic mesh descends upon these our obelisks, steaming in the grip of sycophantic cherub wannabes. This cloverleaf has spanned a half-unconscious message—the gist, you old muleskinner! Her hair caught in grinders. My kissed mouth late to the fountain. The weight of snowflakes forms the other side of the equation (not for the squeamish), so leave it to the courtiers to unpack. Who dwells among us, selling "the diaphanous" by the square foot? Giles, please show the Reader to a gangplank. The huntsman's incantation, freed from its harness, will now go. Mountain laurel. Embolism. The weeks have eaten—swallowed like a pulse on paper or a pattern of bells.

3.

Wax tapirs I'd expected. White writing overhead. The usual hibiscus—flutes and whirlwinds, mortality in velvet cuffs, subpoenas disguised as butcher's aprons recalled from childhood. O the juggler's lisp! How the present informs the past! My name carved in malachite like the snowman's mouth or parentheses of an indeterminate quadrant doubling back. "On bare bones," she said. "On bare bones."

4.

And therefore no hypotaxis. Categorical fixities: “murky realms.” Double horizons’ cracked walls reveal/re-veil etceteras. Broken surface. Wheels click outside the door. Extrapolate swollen tongues to one blue flame. In the gap between “thinking with words” and “letting the words think for you” (or “through you”) dwells this mortal flesh, with its sticks and stones, pleasures and pains. Conflagration of nerves, awaiting the coup de grace. Text of blemishes, death coiled in a beauty mark. “I am nature,” said the artist. Surnames on the breeze. Thinking through and being thought by words, we are constantly re/con/figured. And so it is written. “Etcetera, etcetera.”

5.

Is my koan limping? Mother served bowls of glycerin at the Annual Presbyterian Car Wash, while dirigibles dropped thumbprints on your yearbook picture—hence, these emanations. Purple kenosis. Post hoc abrasions. It is said that hylomorphism washes out with the proper detergent, but few dare put that theorem to the test. Has anyone seen my earmuffs? Does anyone still say "lickety-split," in the vernacular sense? Perhaps if I'd read Abelard's correspondence when I was seventeen, none of this would have fenestrated. Yet my latch collection is beyond reproach. Now, if you don't mind, I will disambiguate your ontology, using these marabou feathers, and—Hey! Who let the penny-whistle salesman in? What am I supposed to do with all these squirting cufflinks? Oh, right.

6.

Hieroglyphic baptisms fester. Welcome to The Nominalist Picnic. Such a deep red—a deep, deep red! Or is it a "red deep"? Either way, "Look out stomach, here it comes!" I chose this sword a priori. Is that all you got? Make it gnu. Make it gnaw. Make it now—or make it numb. How's that for a basement full of heirlooms? These angels use protractors to measure our discomfiture, and so I ask you: Got any doo-dahs to spare? Don't laugh, Janis. Keats might have written this had he lived long enough. Now dittos rise above the steamy lake, and we are submerged in category mistakes. So much for your frog-toed felicity and ironing board bromides! My tears are bluer than yours, anyway. Now pull my finger before Death arrives in his little tugboat, bearing galvanized buckets of chum. I'm dog-starred! I'm also either delirious or deleterious, depending on your choice of codex. Naturally, you picked the red one.

7.

Your trichinosis sunsets. Your prattling fondue. Your septic melancholia. Your flowering inconsequence. These are the reasons—for what, I don't know. Do you mind holding my infinite regress? That the Reformation began on Halloween is purely coincidental. Does the very concept of a thing entail its existence, as per Anselm, or did I pay too much for these indulgences? Kierkegaard said, "I stick my finger into existence. It smells of nothing." I say, "It could be worse." What is that rumbling beneath my god-terms? Sorry, I mean "our" god-terms. When I wake, will my dreams remember me? I am loved for my predictable nature and my facility for subtraction, but what about these claxons? Must you go about defamiliarizing everything? When will my frisson arrive in the mail? Who are you, anyway? Why do I feel faint? Tis an indifferent wind that blows across your left quadrant, or so a little bird told me. Of course, the little bird could be lying. Come to think of it, so could I. *Your narcoleptic garage doors. Your xylophone kisses. Your syllogistic ice trays. Your ambient grief.*

8.

Star-mandibles eat eyes. My physicians call for bloodletting. I remind myself that “drink” is both noun and verb—has anyone seen my scutcheon? Sunlight xylophones down upon the memory of a lake from my mirror’s “wanton youth.” To reach that lake, drive a blue car through valleys of yes and no. Condense. Displace. In dreams begin prehensile tails. My astrologer quotes Aeschylus between sobs, while my physicians call for more leeches. Star-mandibles eat eyes. Morphemes splatter on the windshield. My mesmerist reminds me, “Each symptom begins as a trace.” If only I had my scutcheon! Later that day, I encounter Ludwig Wittgenstein, standing in the checkout line, but he’s too busy counting coupons to answer my questions.

9.

We parted at the palisades. Someone dispensed the pinchable woo. A professional lance-boiler curtailed the phantasmagoria with a wet kiss, into which plumb lines were lowered. Mute expectation gripped us. It was more than met the eye. We searched in vain for moon-mist and sincere explanations, but the mirror's scaffolding came undone. Later, in the ammo shoppe, it occurred to me that if poetry was football, your every poem would line up in a Power-I formation. No wonder my sclera clouds over when the tide comes in. No wonder I'm glacial. Now our sleepy hamlet's agog because someone's been setting carillons on fire; someone's been pouring itching powder in the town crier's shoes; someone's been dunking cuckoo clocks in the haiku pond. No wonder I feel a trepidatious yawn coming on. Say, is that a German accent? I thought I tasted vinegar. Oh well. Thank you for another esophageal evening, Mr. Kooch.

10.

"Amnesia means constant discovery," she cooed, mindlessly stroking her shar-pei. An error-ridden cloud descended on copper wires. I was no longer the fuse-box man. Anarchic clowns stormed the compound and took everyone hostage, forcing us to swallow live goldfish on command, and yet I couldn't help but wonder: how do you keep your intentionality coiled like that? Is there a name for it? Please don't say "Withershins"; it will only trigger my neuropathy. After all, I, too, was once a dreamy haberdasher, writing my thesis on boredom, which I perceived as a gray hum beneath your floorboards, but now your prattle has driven me to distraction: "How do I calculate these dividends? Should I deduct the cost of office supplies from the payroll? What's our amortization schedule?" *Who gives a fuck? Can't you see I'm preoccupied with these forlorn cries of "Illisible" seeping through the porthole?* Besides, it's time to recite some Goethe. If you need me, I'll be in the viper pit. When are the pyrite showers due to arrive? Does my breath smell fishy to you? "Excuse me, but have we even met?" she asked, her voice a dull pedal tone beneath the shar-pei's incessant whining. Our gazes locked, and then a passing cloud of recognition swept across her face. "Wait, don't tell me. Viper pit? Pyrite showers? I *do* know you! Your name is on the tip of my tongue," she exclaimed. *Is it? Is it really?* I gave my jaw harp three good twangs. Outside the window, an error-ridden cloud descended on copper wires. I was no longer the fuse-box man.

11.

Scrawny noumena. The blue cape I wear inside myself spreads wider. Rendezvous in the boiler room. Voices whispering "Surmount." I don't know how the Countess's signet ring wound up in my knapsack, but I keep "writing to find out." So far, no clear theme has emerged. Paucities of custard. Creeping nightshade. The last coefficient is always a remainder. Who invited the moonlight to spread its capricious effluvia all over these crenelations? I've seen plagues slither past us, one by one, disguised as gondoliers. Is it time to dream of flowering hawthorn and butter churns? "Aberrant, not errant"—that's what the deontologist's assistant said. Itchy bellwether. Cobras in my brain pan. Now let's dismount whatever it is we're riding before the road forks and the melodious scent of persimmons overwhelms the lonely drawbridge operator whose raincoat is lost.

12.

I tried your "universal solvent." Now all my dreams are tautological. Fallen angels beset me with their pin cushions of fear and lust as I wander through the pink fog at memory's edge, reciting prokaryotic poems with linguistic blind spots that must be seen to be believed. Or is it "believed to be seen"? One angel, whose eyes resemble yours, reminds me that thermal lag decreases as conductivity increases. "The literal is a closed text," he says, lifting his robe to reveal five roseate wounds haloed with rusty fish-hooks. That's when I pray to a higher power: "Lord, reduce me to a plot device. Whisper perfect circles in my ear. Adjust my zeugma. Lie to me in dreams. Let the solipsistic rose hum with a darker flame as I trap moonlight in a hand mirror and toss desire from red steeples. Teach me to glisten. Make my coefficients sparkle with your Tibetan cleansing bell. Ambush my largesse. Hide algorithms in my beard. Cauterize with false fire these imaginary wounds, then listen to me sing the words that hurt empiricists most." I pause and gaze expectantly skyward. No avail. The angel merely snickers. "I'm not ambidextrous," he replies, as his wounds begin to pulse. "Very well," I say. "Then answer me this: is suffering supposed to be a virtue?" The angel shrugs. "You tell me," he replies, and together we watch our textual selves merge, then fade, like tired parentheses sinking into the loam of a soon-to-be empty page.

13.

Think it through. Think it over. I'm all thought out. I'm lost in the topaz mines. My xylophone succumbs to verdigris, which darkens its tone. Is that you, Mrs. Cavendish? Throw away your tuning fork. Admit impediments. Each day I chew another faulty syllogism; each night I sleep on minted sheets. Would you call that a confession? Bless me, Muses, for I have written. Summer's eye is blinking shut, and the bougainvillea shimmer. Still, I picture you, floating high above your own gestalt, weeping topaz tears, and swapping fictions with a scabrous moon. The ensuing thoughts dissolve my "scholarly ethos." I emit parabolic sighs, wear a zig-zag expression. My dreams overflow with haptic uncertainty. I'm lost in the topaz mines. "As long as there is a straining toward style, there is versification," says Mallarme. Then what about these toadstools on my tongue? What about these razor blades you installed beneath my sternum, claiming they were wind chimes? What about these stained-glass eyelids through which I peer at you, as you coax recalcitrant hosannas from paper boys? Which reminds me, the other day I saw Death strolling through the shopping mall, carrying an hourglass instead of a scythe. I remember wondering, "What difference does that make? I'm still compelled to think allegorically." "Oh yeah? You sure about that, sonny?" hissed the reclusive feather merchant, peeping out from behind her kiosk and blinking uncontrollably. "Maybe you should think harder."

14.

Are some words meant to block our view? What of the mirrors we carry inside us? Is every touch a form of turbulence? Are we always standing on the verge? Now night curdles around us, and the house resumes its whisperings. Your lover counts spiders in her sleep, yet outside the window, real crickets serenade the moon in keening, subliminal tones. How shall we distinguish the object from desire? Does comprehension enter through the gaps? At the end of the corridor, a red door closes. Through its keyhole, a voice that sounds like your dead mother's accuses you of forgetting something important—something on which your very life depends. Voices in memory, voices in dreams. Each distorts the other, the way stained glass makes a liar of the sun. One voice says, "You will never walk in someone else's sleep." The other says, "Have you ever noticed that it's darker when your eyes are open?"

15.

Tongues forked and silver. Whelk-shell ears. Who will spill purple gossip beneath this sycophantic moon? Will it be that ancient chronicler, festooned with skin tags, crouching beneath the trellis? How about Mrs. Bellingham and her ungainly girls from the sewing academy? No? Then let the ventriloquists find honest work! All morning long, sad-colored birds with black chevrons on their wings have been making corkscrew sounds in the skip laurel. At noon, the sea whispered "Death," as usual. Need I remind you that too much self-expression attracts salt vendors? I need someone to swaddle my memory-orb. I need a whir of castanets and an origami swan. I need a hyena-faced god to emerge from the viburnums, approach the podium, and fiddle with this transistor radio until my head fills with sweet gusts of static. Perhaps in the meantime you could wave to the crowd and smile mimetically? Otherwise, they'll accuse these tropes of being "wholly ornamental" again. Folks around here expect their figures to mean something, which usually involves getting their feelings poked with sticks—as long as the sticks are familiar! Otherwise, they'll need a Greek chorus to explain how "concrete historical conjunctions" become "universal aspects of the human condition." So warm up the exargasia. Let's all try to imagine Hell or fathom a skylark. I was born with these zippers, and God willing, I intend to use them!

16.

It broke through the thicket. Sweet longing seized him at heart. Leaked distances. Margins demanding limits. He couldn't see clear to the memory's far side, even with his eyes closed—but then, how could he face that which has no face? Something's stirring beneath the words. Something's waiting to be embodied. Term, terminus, terminal. "Touch me where my shadow attaches." Poem and pearl, word and nacre, born of irritants. The dream brings him closer to awareness. Widening parentheses. Incognito lips. It broke through the thicket. An old woman arrives at dawn, knits his arteries into a shroud. Breathe. *Breathe.* What is the body but the soul's closed fist? "Do you read to find the unspoken word? Is the moon but a vowel in your mouth?" Pleasure and pain are poems the body writes—death an unnamable stone on the tongue.

17.

"Death unties the knot of 'as if,'" says Mr. Kooch. "It disconnects gestures, dissolves dictionaries. It is the sky saying 'Nothing' to itself, the hole in the water from which concentric ripples spread, the already-absent center of which we are the circumference. Have you ever asked yourself why pi is an irrational number and the self a moving cursor, and why, thinking about death—or anything for that matter—you struggle to find the right word?" "Tell him there is no right word," says Mrs. Cavendish, extending a pale finger in what seems to be my direction. Our imaginary eyes lock. She begins to caress my thenar webspace. "There is only the next one and the next one and the next one."

18.

Pluperfect ghosts exit texts gracefully. Ex-lovers dig a trench around my house. Someone's sprinkling rosewater on the apertures, pressing flowers in wax paper, dropping baby teeth in a jar. Have we tasted our fill of wet orchids? Back on the invisible shore, statues streaked with soot gaze sadly at fountains. I study x-rays of the moon, argue prognoses with moths. From behind the mirror, I watch you undress until my next thought burns a hole in itself. A voice on the phone reminds me, "There is a night inside the night, but there is no word inside the word." It's time I acquire a historical sense. Can someone explain why my shadow has grown more pronounced or why my third eye is made of glass? Why is it, whenever I think of you, I bite down on the rind of darkness, expecting it to be bitter, only to find it has no taste at all? Quick—another writing prompt! Inside my head, behind the black curtain, God clears His throat. "I'm coming out now," He says. "You'd better close your eyes."

19.

What shall be done when the death wagon comes ringing its leaden bell and the angels are approaching you with rusty pliers and your lover's eyes turn gray as a Prague sunset in December when the dogcatchers are all on strike and the old woman outside the Eastern Orthodox Church shows her homegrown speckled swan gourd to any passersby willing to stop and listen as she explains that it's shaped exactly like her dead husband's tumor and meanwhile the Tall Man whom you see only peripherally extends his dice stick over your casket in a dream and you're wondering why the carpet cleaner's truck has been parked in the neighbor's driveway for two days with the engine running and the moon is hiding behind Father's eyepatch plotting another coup as your lover nibbles on your aorta the way lovers do in Moravia where the gas shortage has reached its thirteenth month and the shadows speak but only from rote memory while the echoes of the sea find themselves beached at last on an unimagined shore?

20.
I think we're entering another Rose Period. Very well. Pink pills, do your work. Already dawn loosens her garters and daffodils bare their teeth. Death, disguised as a saltimbanque recalled from childhood, wanders the courtyard with his painted birds and wooden flute. Nearby, the old woman from the street corner, who sells emetics by the thimble-full, points a crooked finger at the morning star and winks. Is she looking at me? She spreads wide her black cloak, which I see is lined with pocket watches, all of them gold like my grandfather's, all of them set to 3:33—or frozen there, since the second hands don't seem to be moving. At the sight of her wares, Death begins to sidle toward her, as if drawn by a magnet. And here is the strange thing: I could swear that he is smiling. Of course, since I'm watching everything through a keyhole, I can't be certain.

21.

Someone’s taking a razor to the moon. Someone’s whispering “Onomatopoeia” to the sea. What can I offer you but a dream’s coordinates, a cartographer’s tears, or the torn pages of a poem? One memory always veils another. The body is a bridge between voids. Death wanders through the alphabet’s labyrinth, seeking the letters that will cancel my name. I can feel his lips moving as he reads. Now someone is ringing a white bell in a hailstorm of skeleton keys. Someone is inventing God in a blue garage. In the basement of her father’s shop, the butcher’s deaf-mute daughter paints marionettes in your image. Is she in our heads, or are we in hers? Now I wind a silver timepiece, while around your sleeping form a eunuch choir bleeds lullabies from red, amnesiac mouths.

22.

After all, you can't doubt everything. At the very least, you must be certain that you're doubting. My mirror gets sixty-five channels—how many does your window get? Memory-brine leaves a residue of salt until the tongue turns to coral and the moon's drooping eyelid signals the next aphasia. *I'm sorry I've forgotten your name.* My doctors say I'm "light-headed," not "dizzy" —apparently, there's a difference, and without difference, no diagnosis is possible. Do you doubt it? My mother once told me that my first word was "now." "Such an odd first word for a child," she said. "Not the usual 'mama' or 'dada.' We couldn't understand it, until your grandmother pointed out that every time I talked to you, I preceded each statement with 'now': 'Now it's time for your bottle. Now it's time for your bath. Now we're going for a ride.' No wonder you said it first." Thinking about this many years later, it occurs to me that "now" is the ultimate id-word, a cry for instant gratification: "I want it, and I want it *now*!" "That's right," says Mr. Kooch, "and it leads me to wonder—will your last word be 'then'?" "No," says Mrs. Cavendish. "It will be 'catachresis.'"

23.

I don't want to think about last words. And so I just keep talking. I stir this dream-and-memory soup, hear the clicking of the spoon against my skull. Death rattles. Someone decorated my pineal gland for Christmas. Someone waved goodbye from a blue car. Someone hurled his epaulets from the parapet, then fled to the front in dress shoes. Which color goes best with catalepsy? Is it true that, thinking of you, the translators conversed in rhyme? Now, inside my eyelids, white writing appears, but it's in reverse, so I need a mirror to read it. "Sorry, we're fresh out of mirrors," says the second-string perfusionist, busily arranging loosestrife in a porcelain vase. Who left all these egg cartons? Where I come from, Tuesday is fold-your-wash day. Where I come from, "I" is a god term. Listen, Janis, it doesn't have to end like this—all shrunken noumena and smoldering carillons—, but if it's any consolation, the pink rats are humming our song! Don't mistake the melting snow for tears. Mother's gone—Father, too. Reader, you're still here—I see you in my mind's eye, standing beneath the apple blossoms, a lyre in one hand and an abacus in the other. Will you be my far shore? Will you speak of me in gerunds and pretend I exist? Will you be the place where my doubt begins?

Searching for *Le Mot Au Jus*

1.

Symbology was his overgarment on that ghost-bosomed summer night. She tugged him gently beneath a hieroglyphic moon. "Come down from the Parthenon frieze," she cooed. He awoke drenched in Sappho oil, dropped objective correlatives in the snow. Candle spurts and rosehips—a tawdry bedroom. How do you say "interstitial" in German? A sledgehammer is a good example. His brain made whimpering sounds, polished bannisters in the dark—and still, aesthetics prevailed. The psychiatric panel requisitioned new floodlights. "Dream anything differently," said the mayor of Plastic Babylon, where already the marketplace seemed less than theoretical. We tried to establish eminent domain, knowing that, in the struggle for individualism, confetti is an option. But it was clear that our fashionable days were coming to an end.

2.

Prussian girl-glossing involves chiffon—don't ask me how. Also, don't wake the shooting gallery. Every vicar knows that thigh verbs lolly-fizzle, while stirrups divulge. Vexed colloquialisms. Popular broadheads. We dined on capon and schadenfreude. "That's Bubby's pogo stick," said the freckle-faced juror. Who's ready for a naked centrifuge? He came to amidst fixities of cross-varnish. *How's the old kaboodle?* Pale, very full of grease. Radical dumbwaiters, nostalgic for hand-cranking, communicate telepathically. I was waylaid by a troupe of vertical axis pole-dancers en route to someplace else, someplace more fraternal, less chafed. Don't tell me you *still* don't understand! I want to ride the velvet spiral and untie gray knots. I want to ask French questions and watch bluebells fall from mirrors. Nuances clot in my mouth. The capon is meant to be ironical.

3.

Were you thankful when the silver birds turned translucent? Did we make obtuse catcalls on love's fractal shore? It's time to install a lexicon for soliloquizing. Let each whiplashed heart find its anaphora. Let each true poet read by the light of something "glimpsed recently"—for who among us can enumerate the caramelized slip-knots of emotion? Father always shrugged in a different language. Our little town was known for its stampedes. I had a catch-phrase: "Look for me in the candy gutter," but it never caught on. Some called me "neo-classical," others, a "Lazarus-in-patent leather," others still, "a ward of the state." One thing I knew: a secret kiss lasts a lifetime. Also, this silhouette won't pay the bills.

4.

Who'll vouch for this butter? Am I hormone-compliant? What tastes like sky-backlash? Sharpshooters drop "My Lai poppers" in the vestibule, pardon forgivable glue-sniffers. Titular. Noun-share. Literal winces. Volunteer linchpins visually gulp contracts, knowing Truth's onerous. Well, graze my calypso! "Frictionless" how? Bathtub Handel ricochets milky hoopla and recidivist *kaputs,* over-and-out. She's a practicing Methodist is all I know! Quit the birddog business. Collect apparitional sequins, melancholic déjà vu. To thine own self be skewed. Bubble pulled dilation wax. Cantilevered wad tumult. Root antipathy, leper-sleeved. Pitch white like putty under orders, and don't be a dog-snorer. Wake me twice like an old expression. It's true what they spray: your voice sounds different in print.

5.

Your voice sounds different in print. Are those pitchforks flippant? This room appears nearly empty—and the wrong color, too, albeit one possessing "incredible clarity," as the Neo-Platonists like to say. Everywhere you sense a substitution of feeling for belief. The air quivers with yellow scarves and the tinkling of similar endings. Just ask the man in the dark suit, standing open-mouthed above a harmonium. Clearly, his evanescence is fully automated. He reeks of doppelgangers, and his noir fuse sneers resume-chits. "Stop demanding money to watch you sleep," he chides. But you've already jazzed your ditto-hunch. Besides, nothing peripheral out-gavels a lush string accompaniment, even if it's factory-sealed. You can smack-dab that notion with your stumpy luger.

6.

Sleepover nimbus. Vibrato in cashmere. Slur verbatim sock-hop tourniquet. Going to stutter-bomb the tenderloin, confer tertiary handcuff cream. "Ad hoc," she said. Words cracked open, pheromone-secreting clubhouse. Arrest bondage chocolate. Prerecorded fall guy, gooey anti-Christ escapes prism. I took a course in Chemical Linguistics—suggest you do the same, spiny human. Don't be so anal-inventive. Simulated cockpit bullion, sticker price tremens notwithstanding. Not a dry iamb in the house. Call it "lilac fatalism" or call it "pirate jelly"—either way, it's plum subtraction. Shall we roger that? Do I hear a second? Your simulacra left a stain, by the way. Sorry. I smell "substitutive systems," you old spin-doctor you, and so I must exit, pursued by a hair. If you get lonely, look for me in the candy gutter.

7.

Backseat-amok on point. Curious dints. Was she polyglot? Blue toads divulged, and a fellow would harness milkshakes. Unrelenting B-movie signature-husk: treble bore. Detonate frenzies. Less travelled prom-flavored compromise, silently stalking. Guess we're due for a standstill. Meanwhile, Nigel succumbed to pew dilation because some fool jiggled the touché-switch. Let's face it: teeth chattering with "social undecidability" wet no fiscal whistles. That's Flaubert for you! He slept through the hole thing. Now I detect signals from the thorny precipice, oozing tithe-glitter and squeegee remorse. Why can't you tell her the page is upside down? That "lyrical I" ain't nothin' but a pronoun, promise-crammed—a two-stepping preemie in the ever-pixilated dark, with lack-of-plenum and a bad case of itch-by-proxy. Just ask my allergist if you don't believe me.

8.

Puppet band, beset with pendulum-cramps. Gratuitous puff. Monkey barrel squint-grease (pie latent) effervesces Mom's gesundheit. Dry sod and dry chaff. Vile squirt miscarriage. Mouthpiece-swallowed milk prong breeds lullaby verdict. Expedite the lulu! Corn-feed that nostrum! Who says I'm de-centered? "Explain it to the nice people." *Not the right word but the juiciest one!* Windex the diaphanous? We don't do windows. Please excuse our "language-poet-hubris-dust" while we are under construction. What maintains? Catapulting beef renewal. Sentimental sprocket latency, ground to indeterminacy. Who ordered fufu? It's like the mall kiosk shaman said: "Maybe you should try rhyme."

9.

Lose good. Seize her. Eye blink silo. Espouse his sin, eh? Pillage. Throw keys. Shrill knot's seedy droppings—mere blue "crotch-biz" could still cup. Fifth row. Sigh piddle course, dust-stink adhere. Boo flop. Myth pout a harmed douse. Beer between. Huh would sand flow, then take? The spark nest, Steve! Fling of the weary. Sieve this. Far nest. Fella breaks new flask. Whiff hair whiz. Dumbest flake. The lonely mother mound. The creep-shove. Measly gin and greasy steak. Ma should love me—hearken, sheep! Smut-eye got prom dresses. Screwed deep—and files due! Show me, four-eyes! Deep-end style's too slow! Restore my sleep.

10.

Walleye Tom wears see-through. The slumber weighs out. Darts or doves? Eating your desperate muffins. Who fakes a farthing? Suds dismay. And rubber-sleeved "Plath dolls" report irate windchimes. Two tots deny eleven. Wines can soften "business." Old confections skimmed Fran's savory faire. Compare dumb rhymes. Decline thigh-dancer's play. Your cage's door's unhinged. Smut-eye burns all! Strum her trill knot. Trade four screws. No messin' with cat hairs. Bow lowest. Bore gall-breathed hags. Now pawns dress in frizzed suede. Bending intern will dine on limes. Alto tests show wrong jazz when all give planned sighs. Balmy "kabong!" sieves this sand, misgives night duty.

www.ingramcontent.com/pod-product-compliance
Lightning Source LLC
La Vergne TN
LVHW010108110826
845155LV00028B/546